Robert Oppenheimer
1904–1967

Robert F. Bacher

Professor of Physics
California Institute of Technology

Monograph 2

The Los Alamos Story

Robert Oppenheimer 1904-1967
Second Printing
Printed in the United States of America

All rights reserved. No part of this book may be reproduced or transmitted in any form of by any means, electronic or mechanical, including photocopying, recording, or by any information storage or retrieval system without written permission from the publisher, except for the inclusion of brief quotations in review.

Photographs courtesy of Los Alamos National Laboratory and Los Alamos Historical Society.

Design and layout by Gloria Sharp.

Library of Congress Cataloging-in-Publication Data
Bacher, Robert F(ox), 1905-
Judy Gursky, Editor
Robert Oppenheimer / Robert F. Bacher
P. CM. -- (The Los Alamos Story; monograph 2)
ISBN 0-941232-22-0
1. Oppenheimer, J. Robert, 1904-1967. 2. Atomic bomb--United States--History. 3. Physicists--United States--Biography.
I. Title. II. Series.
QC16.062B33 1999
530'.092--dc21

[B]

99-26500

CIP

Copyright © 1999
Los Alamos Historical Society
Box 43, Los Alamos, New Mexico 87544

Robert Oppenheimer

A small group of young people, most in their 20s and 30s, met near the middle of the twentieth century on an isolated mesa far from the sights and sounds of the rest of the world. Working closely together for two and a half years on a secret, single-focus mission, they brought about the most significant technology of their century, creating a watershed event that would produce profound changes to be felt not only in their own country and at a specific time but in the entire world and for all time.

When their mission, to produce the atomic bomb, was completed, many of the scientists and others who had done this work decided to stay here in what had been a muddy army post beset with water shortages, difficulties in transportation and communication, inadequate housing, as well as other hardships. Those who stayed would be joined by others, and together they would create a community worthy of its first reason for being and of the natural beauty in which it was embraced. Business and medical people, teachers, construction workers, clergy, all joined the scientists in building schools and churches, a hospital, a library, parks and places for sports activities, businesses, streets, attractive neighborhoods.

The Los Alamos Historical Society has continued to collect and preserve memories and facts of every kind from the beginning--photographs, oral histories, physical objects, journals, reports. Now, near the end of the century and into the beginning of the next, the Society's Publications Division sets out on the journey to make accessible many of these facts and artifacts in a series of one-subject monographs grouped together under the title, *The Los Alamos Story*.

Robert Oppenheimer

As the second in its series of monographs, *The Los Alamos Story*, the Los Alamos Historical Society has selected a biographical memoir of Robert Oppenheimer by his close friend and colleague, Robert F. Bacher. The unique story of the wartime development of the atomic bomb at Los Alamos is personified by "Oppie" and his remarkably successful leadership.

Bacher and Oppenheimer first met in 1930. After Oppenheimer was appointed to lead the Manhattan Project laboratory at Los Alamos, he brought in Bacher as head of the Experimental Physics Division and later of the Bomb Physics Division. In the years following the war Bacher was closely associated with Oppenheimer as Bacher served on the Atomic Energy Commission and the President's Scientific Advisory Committee. In this memoir, he tells of Oppenheimer's life and character, his scientific accomplishments, his crucial wartime leadership and postwar security problems.

This biography was first published in The Proceedings of the American Philosophical Society, vol 116, No. 4, August, 1972. It is reprinted with the permission of Robert F. Bacher and the American Philosophical Society.

Robert Oppenheimer

We, like all men, are among those who bring a little light to the vast unending darkness of man's life and world. For us as for all men, change and eternity, specialization and unity, instrument and final purpose, community and individual man alone, complementary each to the other, both require and define our bonds and our freedom.

Robert Oppenheimer died in Princeton, New Jersey, on February 18, 1967, at the age of sixty-two. He was the leading American theoretical physicist of his generation, the founder of the most important school of theoretical physics, and one of the leading intellectuals of our day.

Robert Oppenheimer

Early Years

Robert Oppenheimer, whose full name was J. Robert Oppenheimer, was born in New York City on April 22, 1904. His father, Julius Oppenheimer, was a very successful member of a firm of textile importers which had been started by his uncle and which his father had joined at an early age after immigrating from Germany. His mother, Ella Friedman Oppenheimer, shared her husband's interest in the Ethical Culture Society and had many interests of her own. She was an accomplished painter. Robert grew up in an atmosphere of culture and affluence in which his intellectual curiosity was stimulated and encouraged. At a very early age he became interested in minerals and by age eleven was a member of the New York Mineralogical Club, largely on the basis of an erudite correspondence which he carried on with some of the members.

Robert grew up in an atmosphere of culture and affluence in which his intellectual curiosity was stimulated and encouraged.

Robert attended the Ethical Culture School in New York where he apparently kept much to himself, having little interaction with other students. He had great facility with languages and before he graduated he had mastered several languages as well as almost everything else the school had to offer. His family had long before recognized him as a prodigy and fed his voracious appetite for learning with books about his latest interests. His interests moved toward chemistry and he had the good fortune to have a stimulating teacher, Augustus Klock.

During the summers the family would move to a house in Bay Shore on the south shore of Long Island. His father presented him with a sailboat which Robert

J. Robert Oppenheimer

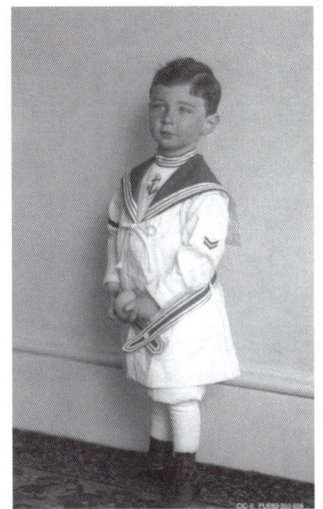

Robert Oppenheimer as a child with his mother and father.

3

Robert Oppenheimer

Robert and his brother Frank

. . . his father persuaded one of his former instructors at Ethical Culture School to go west with him to a ranch in the upper Pecos area of the Sangre de Cristo Mountains in New Mexico

named *Trimethy* after a chemical compound that interested him. He and his younger brother Frank, born in 1912, sailed the Great South Bay endlessly. He became an accomplished sailor and kept an interest in sailing for the rest of his life.

In spite of outdoor summers, Robert was frail and was often ill, especially during the winters. He completed his work at Ethical Culture School early in 1921 and then took some advanced chemistry before the close of the spring term and graduation. After that his family went to Europe where Robert and Frank had a fine time exploring and seeing the sights. Robert became ill apparently with dysentery and was brought home to recover and recuperate. By fall he had not acquired sufficient strength to enter Harvard where he had been admitted. Instead he stayed in New York and then his father persuaded one of his former instructors at Ethical Culture School to go west with him to a ranch in the upper Pecos area of the Sangre de Cristo Mountains in New Mexico. Katherine Page, who owned and operated this ranch, encouraged Robert's interest in the outdoors and riding. He rapidly gained strength and after spending the summer again at Bay Shore, headed for Harvard with enthusiasm.

Heading Into Physics

To quote his own words he "almost came alive" at Harvard. He was able to start with advanced standing and each year audited more courses (including examinations) than he took regularly. He soon realized that his interests were in physics and was attracted to Percy Bridgman, who gave him help and good advice. Robert Oppenheimer graduated *summa cum laude* in three years.

The next year he went to Cambridge University where he tried his hand at some experiments. He was greatly attracted by visiting lecturers who were reporting on the new work in quantum mechanics, especially Max Born. As a result, he transferred to Göttingen and immediately found himself in the midst of an extraordinary group of professors, postdoctoral fellows and students who were deep in the application of the new quantum mechanics. Robert worked with great intensity and with such success that in the spring of 1927 after less than two years he was awarded the Ph.D degree.

He was greatly attracted by visiting lecturers who were reporting on the new work in quantum mechanics, especially Max Born.

For the following year he had a National Research Council fellowship at Harvard and the California Institute of Technology. By this time he had made some major contributions in the application of the new quantum mechanics and was widely sought after for a university position. He decided that he needed another year to study before he started to teach and he was awarded an International Education Board fellowship to study in Europe at Leiden and at Zurich. Paul Ehrenfest and especially Wolfgang Pauli made deep impressions on him.

Robert Oppenheimer

At this point he expressed a strong desire to go home. He had decided on an unusual arrangement of a double appointment as assistant professor at Caltech and at the University of California at Berkeley. For several years he taught through the fall term at Berkeley, then after Christmas went to Pasadena for the spring. His teaching was not an immediate success. He felt that he was going much too slowly; yet his students had real difficulty keeping up the pace. In addition, he spoke very softly with a fair amount of mumbling. This once caused Ehrenfest, a stickler for clear exposition, to call repeatedly in a Caltech seminar, "Louder, please, dear Oppenheimer." When Robert's voice quickly dropped after the third call he banged his desk. Robert stopped and said, "But this room is so big." Ehrenfest shouted, "You always adjust your voice so we can't hear. I couldn't hear you in a telephone booth." Before very many years Robert Oppenheimer became an excellent lecturer and many of his general lectures are known for their lucid expositions of fundamental ideas in physics.

Before very many years Robert Oppenheimer became an excellent lecturer and many of his general lectures are known for their lucid expositions of fundamental ideas in physics.

Leadership in Theoretical Physics

Students were attracted to Robert Oppenheimer and he soon established a group of students and postdoctoral fellows with whom he worked. Their relation with him was close and personal. When he went to Pasadena in the spring most of his group followed along. Some too, followed him to his ranch in the upper Pecos, a beautiful spot not far from where he had stayed before and which he had acquired before going to Europe in 1928. He called it "Perro Caliente," Hot Dog, reputedly the exclamation he made when he first saw it. Through the thirties his summers were almost always spent there in New Mexico. He used it as a base from which he and his brother Frank took long rides through the mountains and high desert for days at a time. It was a vigorous life and doubtless helped to develop the extraordinary stamina which he showed later. Many visitors, especially his students and physicist friends, visited there and had lively discussions on new work in quantum theory.

Robert Oppenheimer gradually shortened his visits to Caltech and made Berkeley his main base. Just before World War II he lived almost entirely in Berkeley except for occasional visits and a few weeks in the early summer in Pasadena. He had many friends in Pasadena and always kept a close interest in the work in cosmic rays and high-energy radiation, since it was so close to his longtime theoretical interests. During the years before the war, Robert Oppenheimer's group in theoretical physics was the strongest one in the country. In addition to excellent graduate students, numerous postdoctoral fellows, including Julian Schwinger, Robert Serber, and many others, worked with him. It was a vigorous and productive group and former members now staff many of the most distinguished university faculties in theoretical physics.

Kitty Oppenheimer, Robert's wife

In 1940 Robert Oppenheimer married Katherine Puening Harrison, whom he had met in Pasadena. In 1941 they had their first child, Peter, in Pasadena. About this time Robert bought a house at 1 Eagle Hill which commanded a fine view over San Francisco Bay and which provided a delightful spot to entertain his students and co-workers.

The Start of Weapons Related Fission Research

In late 1940 and early 1941, many of Robert's colleagues left to work on weapons research for a war in which the United States was not yet involved but might soon be.

The discovery of nuclear fission in 1939 tied into many current activities in the Radiation Laboratory at Berkeley, where neptunium and later plutonium were discovered not long after. The fall of France and the battle of Britain began to displace the overpowering concern for research in Berkeley. In late 1940 and early 1941, many of Robert's colleagues left to work on weapons research for a war in which the United States was not yet involved but might soon be.

Some work continued on the fission project which was financed on a relatively small scale by the government through a committee. In early 1942 work on the possibility of producing a nuclear chain reaction was brought together at the Metallurgical Laboratory of the University of Chicago and given greater support. The director, Arthur Compton, asked Robert Oppenheimer to get a theoretical group together in the summer of 1942 to look into the possibility of whether, if reasonably pure fissionable material were available, an explosive could be made, and if so how. Work on the electromagnetic separation process was being undertaken at the Radiation Laboratory in Berkeley under the driving leadership of Ernest Lawrence, who asked Robert to help with some of the separation magnet design problems. It seemed almost an impossible job to get fissionable material in quantity by this method but it was certainly possible in principle. Other methods had even more fundamental difficulties.

By mid-1942 the work by Enrico Fermi and others at Chicago on the possibility of a nuclear chain reaction looked very promising. The first self-sustaining nuclear chain reaction was achieved on December 2, 1942. Although the problems seemed almost insurmountable, this opened the real possibility that plutonium might be produced in quantity as an alternative to uranium 235 as a fissionable material.

Although the problems seemed almost insurmountable, this opened the real possibility that plutonium might be produced in quantity as an alternative to uranium 235 as a fissionable material.

The Manhattan Project Begins

The advances of the uranium project, especially Fermi's work, supplemented by urging from the British, prompted Vannevar Bush and James Conant who held the top responsibility to seek much broader support from President Roosevelt. If anything were to be accomplished here, large industrial plants would be needed and these must be planned immediately and started as soon as possible even before many technical problems were solved. A new project, the Manhattan Project, was created with the highest priorities and Colonel Leslie Groves was put in charge. Actually the organization started earlier but was formally set up in September, 1942, just after Groves was made brigadier general.

Groves was a very fortunate choice to head this project. He was energetic and forceful but very blunt. He was a good judge of people, knew when to trust advice and when he did, he backed that advice without

Robert Oppenheimer

wavering. Heads of the projects aimed at U-235 and plutonium production were already selected: Lawrence for the electromagnetic method, Harold Urey for the diffusion method, and Arthur Compton for the nuclear reactors or piles as they were then called. While Groves was put in charge of production, it was soon agreed that he should take total responsibility including research and development with a Military Policy Committee including Bush and Conant. Not long thereafter, Groves appointed Conant and Richard Tolman as his scientific advisers. Tolman, especially, followed the project closely and provided a link to the scientific community.

This decision certainly took a great deal of insight and nerve because Robert did not have any administrative experience and had never directed anything. It was a brilliant choice.

Groves consulted Oppenheimer about the status of the theoretical studies of the assembly of sufficient fissionable material to make a bomb and what would be the expected effects of the resulting explosion. Oppenheimer pointed out many of the basic unknowns, among them being the wide limits that must be placed on the amount of valuable material needed. He recommended to Groves that proper studies could only be conducted if a separate laboratory were established for this purpose and if there were free exchange among those working on the overall problem. Groves was a strong believer in compartmentalization for this highly secret project. He liked the idea of separating the bomb work from the rest of the project but recoiled at the idea of no compartmentalization within such a laboratory. Groves also had to find a director for such a laboratory. He apparently discussed this at length with Bush and Conant and with the heads of the other projects. There were not many suitable candidates and such as there were had major responsibilities elsewhere. Groves had

Robert Oppenheimer

been greatly impressed by Oppenheimer and decided that if a separate laboratory were to be established, he would make a good director. This decision certainly took a great deal of insight and nerve because Robert did not have any administrative experience and had never directed anything. It was a brilliant choice.

Rio Grande near Los Alamos

   In the fall, steps were taken to locate the laboratory. A site in southern California was examined but Groves thought it was insufficiently isolated. New Mexico was suggested and Groves sent members of his staff to investigate. Finally on a trip with Oppenheimer, Edwin McMillan, and some of his staff, Groves drove over the Jemez Mountains to the site of the Los Alamos Ranch School high on a mesa west of the Rio Grande and close to the Jemez Mountains. This site was sufficiently isolated for Groves and appealed to Oppenheimer, who knew the country well. Water was limited but Groves thought a supply could be found, and steps were taken to acquire a large site.

Robert Oppenheimer

Assembling a Laboratory at Los Alamos

With the assistance of John Manley, who had been helping Oppenheimer with the project almost ever since Compton had given him his first responsibility in this area, and of Edwin McMillan, he started to draw up requirements for a laboratory that would be adequate for about one hundred scientists and engineers. Equipment was borrowed from several universities in order to get a working laboratory as quickly as possible. Oppenheimer spent a great deal of his time recruiting. He had been persuaded by Groves that this undertaking must be a military project with the director an officer. Robert was dismayed to find that those who had experience in war projects declared vigorously that this would not work. After a good deal of discussion it was agreed that the laboratory would start out as a civilian laboratory reporting to Groves but would probably become a military laboratory when significant amounts of fissionable material began to arrive. This was formalized in a letter signed by Groves and Conant.

Fortunately several small groups that had been working on problems associated with the Metallurgical Laboratory in Chicago could be closed down now, and, if the personnel involved could be persuaded, might form a nucleus of a staff for Los Alamos. Robert was very persuasive. The largest number came from Princeton where Robert Wilson with a small group had been working on an alternative

From top: John Manley, George Kistiakowsky, Ernest Lawrence, Enrico Fermi, Isidor Rabi, and Hans Bethe

electromagnetic method of isotope separation. Others came from Berkeley, Illinois, Cornell, Minnesota, Purdue, Chicago, and Wisconsin. Robert attracted a very strong theoretical group centered around those who had worked with him during the summer of 1942 and including Hans Bethe, Edward Teller, Victor Weisskoff, Emil Konopinski, Robert Serber, George Placzek, Robert Marshak, Robert Christy, and Richard Feynman. It was an outstanding group.

The building went up with incredible speed, being made for the most part out of green lumber from trees cut down nearby. By mid-March of 1943 staff members started arriving and were forced to live off-site. By early April the laboratory was sufficiently complete that a conference to pull together all the known information pertinent to the bomb project was scheduled for April 15. The conferees were almost entirely committed project members but there were a few others, including Fermi, without whom any conference on chain reactions would not have been complete, and Isidor Rabi and Robert Bacher from the Massachusetts Institute of Technology Radiation Laboratory (Radar) who had been advising Oppenheimer since the end of 1942 on problems which a new laboratory might encounter. Subsequently a dozen or more members of the MIT laboratory came to Los Alamos, bringing with them technology which had been developed there and which might be helpful at Los Alamos. Members of other war

Technical Area around Ashley Pond, 1940's

Robert Oppenheimer

laboratories also came to Los Alamos and the assembled group represented wide experience in new technical developments.

The conference lasted about ten days. A primer on the subject had been prepared and all of the known information was discussed at length. The preferred method of assembling a supercritical mass with adequate speed was discussed by Serber and others. The idea was to shoot a piece of U-235 into another piece which was surrounded with neutron reflector, or tamper as it was called, at such speed that no neutron reaction would be initiated until the entire mass was highly supercritical. Other methods of assembly were discussed, especially an implosion method which Seth Neddermeyer discussed. The ordnance people were disturbed at the problems that this would raise and had major doubts that a sufficiently symmetrical implosion could be achieved. The gun method looked much easier provided there were no really serious surprises among the many unknown nuclear properties of U-235 and plutonium. Through all of this, Robert Oppenheimer furnished a very skillful guiding hand. He had a tremendous ability to put his finger on critical issues and his clarity of summary after a complicated discussion often made the difference between moving forward and backward. These were qualities which he demonstrated over and over as the laboratory director.

Street scene, Technical Area

Clearance and Other Problems

During this same period, Robert Oppenheimer was having other difficulties. These were not known to his associates but greatly concerned General Groves and some of his staff. These were clearance problems. During the thirties, Robert had many left-wing friends. He had supported the Spanish Loyalists through communist channels but had drifted away from these connections when the flip-flopping communist line made no sense to him. Of course, clearance was required of the director of the Los Alamos Laboratory and the security people must have jumped out of their skins at his record. Clearance had been hanging fire ever since his first association with the project. No security officer would recommend his clearance. Finally General Groves reviewed the case carefully and on July 20, 1943, instructed the security officers to issue a clearance "irrespective of the information which you have concerning Mr. Oppenheimer. He is absolutely essential to the project."

The problems that Robert Oppenheimer had in getting the Los Alamos Laboratory started covered every conceivable subject. Living in an isolated spot and unable to travel except nearby was an entirely new experience for most laboratory staff people. The problems of getting the necessary equipment for the laboratories on very short notice and with such a complicated communication system with the outside world were unbelievable. To solve these and at the same time keep a close watch on the essential substantive problems of the project was almost too much. But Robert did it and at the same time kept a

Finally General Groves reviewed the case carefully and on July 20, 1943, instructed the security officers to issue a clearance "irrespective of the information which you have concerning Mr. Oppenheimer. He is absolutely essential to the project."

Robert Oppenheimer

close personal touch with most of the work going on and the people who were doing it in those early days. Robert had great stamina and although he lost weight and was much too thin, he could outlast almost anyone on the project.

During that first summer of 1943, Robert often expressed privately his real doubts about his suitability for the director's job and his concern as to whether he could really do it. In a sense he was riding the tiger and he felt very heavily pressed by the many problems of the project and doubtless also by his difficulties with the security people. It was perfectly clear to the members of his laboratory that he was doing a superb job no matter how much they would complain about the slowness of getting equipment, the irregularity of power or the difficulties in living in this remote encampment.

Badge photo

During the remainder of 1943 and early 1944 the laboratory made real advances in determining the needed nuclear cross sections of fissionable and other materials for the bomb. Information was also obtained about the number of neutrons emitted per fission and some limits, not adequate but encouraging, on the time after fission when neutrons were emitted. One basic study brought forth some very disturbing information. It was known that U-238 fissioned spontaneously but the rate was sufficiently low that the gun method of assembly of a highly supercritical mass was still believed to be adequate. Emilio Segrè had set up equipment in a remote location to measure the rates of spontaneous fission or at least to put upper limits on them. It was a difficult and painstaking job but a much needed one. At first the amounts of plutonium available were infinitesimal and these were all produced by cyclotron bombardment. Material was soon received from the first intermediate power reactor located at Oak Ridge and Segré found indisputably that this material had a higher spontaneous fission than previously observed with uranium or plutonium. Ordinary impurities, of course, would not produce such an effect and this was believed to be a fundamental property of reactor-produced plutonium due to neutron capture by Pu-239 to produce Pu-240 in the high neutron flux of the reactor. This would inevitably be much worse in the material from the production reactors under construction at Hanford.

It was a project crisis. With the expected spontaneous fission rates, plutonium for a bomb could not be assembled by the gun method. If plutonium was to be used, another method must be found. The only likely method was the implosion method which Neddermeyer and a small group had been working on since the start of the laboratory. Their experiments had shown promise but also many difficulties, especially in trying to find out what was going on in the very short time during the explosion and inward shock. After consideration and consultation with the Governing Board, Robert decided to make a complete reorganization of the laboratory, establishing new divisions and putting more emphasis on the study of explosives and throwing much of the technical experience of the laboratory into the measurements of sample implosions. No one could be sure where this would lead but it was an all-out effort.

With increased effort and the ingenuity shown by Neddermeyer, Donald Kerst, Darol Froman, Alvin

It was perfectly clear to the members of his laboratory that he was doing a superb job no matter how much they would complain about the slowness of getting equipment, the irregularity of power or the difficulties in living in this remote encampment.

Graves, Bruno Rossi, Hans Staub, Edwin McMillan, Edward Creutz, Charles Critchfield, Charles Barnes, and a host of other experimenters, information began to accumulate much faster. Explosives improved and new ideas for their use were developed by George Kistiakowsky and the greatly strengthened division working with him on this problem. These new results provided new information for the theorists who were now able to study both the course of the implosion and the subsequent nuclear explosion which they had studied for the gun method. There were many crises during the winter of 1944 and the spring of 1945 but the work moved forward and showed promise.

The schedule for the test was such that as soon as the plutonium or the bomb was ready, everything else should be ready and the test would be held.

Testing the Bomb and Using It

It had been concluded that a full scale nuclear test of the implosion weapon might be necessary and this was made definite during the winter of 1944-1945. This project, named Trinity, was itself a major undertaking and Kenneth Bainbridge was put in charge of it. He, with the help of others, found a site on the Alamogordo bombing range and preparations for the test went forward both there and at Los Alamos. Now Oppenheimer had even more to worry about and to administer.

The schedule for the test was such that as soon as the plutonium for the bomb was ready, everything else should be ready and the test would be held. There was a little delay but not much. Instructions from Washington were that no day was to be lost and it wasn't. The nuclear assembly and final explosives were completed at Alamogordo and the shot was scheduled for July 16. This was a difficult period for everybody but particularly for Robert Oppenheimer. There were now not only the nuclear problems to worry about but, even worse, the possibility that some electrical failure would ruin the test. On top of everything else it rained in various spots throughout the test site during the night of July 15. In spite of this it was decided to go ahead. The weather prospects for the future were uncertain at this time of year and it was clear to some at least that everyone was so tired that a postponement would of necessity be for several days.

At the test Robert was thin, worn, and bone-tired, but he kept going and functioning very well. He was at the same time jubilant that it had worked and produced such a big explosion, and concerned at the terrible forces now unleashed on the world. But these were concerns that he had thought about before and he knew that the final decisions on use of the bomb must be made by President Truman, considering what the alternatives would be for the next stages of the war in the Pacific.

Oppenheimer and Brig. Gen. Leslie Groves at Point Zero after the Trinity test.

Robert Oppenheimer

The bombs on Hiroshima and Nagasaki caused Robert and many others great sadness. Some scientists thought that a demonstration would be adequate. Robert and many others had doubts that this would work. The decision, of course, had to be the President's.

Most of the staff members at Los Alamos were on leave from positions elsewhere "for the duration" and it was natural that they would soon begin to leave. Robert Oppenheimer made plans to return to California, actually this time to Pasadena, and Norris Bradbury was to succeed him as director. Before he left, a public ceremony was held to make an award to the laboratory. The citation given by General Groves was most complimentary and Robert's reply gave indication of the thoughts that would guide his actions for many years to come:

The peoples of this world must unite or they will perish. This war, which has ravaged so much of the earth, has written these words. The atomic bomb has spelled them out for all men to understand.

The peoples of this world must unite or they will perish. This war, which has ravaged so much of the earth, has written these words. The atomic bomb has spelled them out for all men to understand. Other men have spoken them, in other times, of other wars, of other weapons. They have not prevailed. There are some, misled by a false sense of history, who hold that they will not prevail today. It is not for us to believe that. By our works we are committed, committed to a world united, before this common peril, in law and in humanity.

Attempts to Establish International Control of Atomic Energy

After leaving Los Alamos, Robert Oppenheimer's scientific interest immediately went back to the role of the meson in the origin of nuclear forces. He had followed the work of Carl Anderson and Seth Neddermeyer before the war and realized that the "mesotron" which they had found did not interact with nuclei very strongly. Here was a basic dilemma. He was immediately in demand to lecture far more than he possibly could, on the future role of atomic energy, on the nature and organization of its development in the United States for peaceful purposes, and most of all on how the newly developed bomb could serve to diminish the likelihood of wars.

In November 1945, the American Philosophical Society and the National Academy of Sciences held in Philadelphia a joint symposium on "Atomic Energy and its Implications." Oppenheimer, who had been elected a member of the Society in the spring of 1945, contributed to the symposium a discussion of atomic weapons. No one who heard him ever forgot the eloquence and deep emotion with which he pictured the destructiveness of the bomb or the force of his call for international control of this new awesome development.

The newly established United Nations set up an Atomic Energy Commission, and a high-level committee was established with Under-Secretary of State Dean Acheson as chairman to prepare a position for the United States. This was a difficult and complicated job, and to get it done a full time Board

No one who heard him ever forgot the eloquence and deep emotion with which he pictured the destructiveness of the bomb or the force of his call for international control of this new awesome development.

Robert Oppenheimer

of Consultants was set up with David Lilienthal as chairman. Robert Oppenheimer was a member of this board and its assignment was the subject that he thought most crucial, the international control of atomic energy. The Board went into continuous session and by mid-March had prepared a report which was wide-sweeping in its recommendations. The "Report on the International Control of Atomic Energy," usually referred to as the Acheson-Lilienthal report, proposed an international agency which through several stages would eventually come into control of all atomic developments including the production of raw material, the separation of U-235, the production of plutonium, the production and control of weapons, and the ownership of the whole project.

Secretary of War presenting the Medal of Merit to Oppenheimer, 1946

Robert Oppenheimer played a major role in working out the nature of the proposals and the preparation of the report. The Acheson Committee in passing the report on to the Secretary of State, said:

> We lay the report before you as the Board has submitted it to us, "not as a final plan, but as a place to begin, a foundation on which to build." In our opinion it furnishes the most constructive analysis of the question of international control we have seen and a definitely hopeful approach to

a solution of the entire problem. We recommend it for your consideration as representing the framework within which the best prospects for both security and development of atomic energy for peaceful purposes may be found.

This report received support from many members of the government and others, especially scientists who had worked on the Manhattan project. There were some scientists and a good many members of the military who viewed the report with deep suspicion in spite of the recommendations for a series of stages and provision for detailed inspection. There were some who thought such a plan would never be internationally acceptable, especially to the Soviets.

President Truman appointed Bernard Baruch as representative on the United Nations Atomic Energy Commission and Richard Tolman became his chief scientific adviser. Robert Oppenheimer and several others served as scientific advisers, but Robert had major concern that the Baruch proposal to eliminate the veto would in fact give the Soviets an excuse not to agree. No political progress was made and it took almost the entire summer of 1946 to get the Soviets to agree that international control was technically feasible. In retrospect it seems clear that the Soviets had no intention of agreeing, especially since they were well along on the development of their own project with significant help from espionage on both the United States and British projects. Robert Oppenheimer saw his hope that the bomb would provide the impetus for new international agreement vanishing and he was disheartened by the Soviet introduction of the "Iron Curtain," a move in the opposite direction.

In retrospect it seems clear that the Soviets had no intention of agreeing, especially since they were well along on the development of their own project with significant help from espionage on both the United States and British projects.

The Atomic Energy Commission

During this same time a great debate was going on about the management of the atomic energy project in the United States. The first proposal had been the May-Johnson bill which seemed repressive to many and to be too much involved with the military establishment. Many scientists actively opposed this bill and Robert was criticized by them for his initial support of it. He seemed to feel at the end of the war that any plan which could go into action would be better than no plan and an interval of no action.

General Advisory Committee of the A.E.C.: J.B. Conant, J.R. Oppenheimer, (chairman), Brig. General McCormack, Hartley Rowe, John Manley, I.I. Rabi, Roger Warner.

A bill providing for a civilian commission of five full-time members, the McMahon bill, was passed in the summer of 1946. This bill had been vigorously supported by the Federation of American Scientists and Robert approved of it but was perturbed at the delay. The bill provided for a Military Liaison Committee and for a General Advisory Committee to advise the Commission especially on scientific and technical problems, but since these questions were often tied closely to long-range policies, the scope was very broad. The Commission was appointed in the fall and started work in early November. A General Advisory Committee (GAC) was appointed by the President on recommendation by the Commission and Robert Oppenheimer became one of its members. The

Commission formally took over the management of the Manhattan Project on January 1, 1947, and the GAC held its first meeting almost immediately.

Robert Oppenheimer was elected chairman of the Committee and continued in this position until the expiration of his term in 1952. The Commission was faced with long hearings on the confirmation of its members and with serious problems in setting up a proper system for the clearance of personnel for work which was classified under the Atomic Energy Act. There was at that time very little recourse for the individual whose clearance was denied or revoked by other government agencies, and a new system was developed which was generally regarded as being fairest to the individual. The General Advisory Committee immediately dug into some of the long-range plans. There were serious problems in several of the laboratories due to the exodus of personnel at the end of the war. Nowhere was this more serious than at Los Alamos, and it was a major and urgent problem for the Commission. The GAC clearly recognized the current situation and was most helpful in its correction. There were so many things that needed doing that some had to be postponed and the GAC worked thoughtfully in relating current activities to long-range activities.

Through all of this Robert Oppenheimer made major contributions as a member and chairman of the Committee. He had wider experience than anyone else in the project as a whole and especially with the

Robert Oppenheimer

An enumeration of the major recommendations of GAC would be a long document and all these were enhanced by the effective personal interaction of GAC with the Commission, especially effective with Robert as chairman.

weapons work. There were others who had greater experience in particular areas of the project and greater background in technical management. Robert's clarity in summation of complicated situations was most helpful. He could summarize and formulate a recommendation that took into account varying points of view to the satisfaction of all concerned and which definitely contributed constructively to the solution of the problem. In his conduct of the GAC, he was inclined to listen to all views and reserve his thoughts to the end. Very often he stayed after the meeting for a day to prepare statements of the agreed positions with the needed background and formulation of the problem. All GAC members worked hard and Robert Oppenheimer worked harder than anyone else. The contributions of the GAC under his chairmanship to the work of AEC were major ones in all the scientific and technical areas and especially in the formulation of plans. An enumeration of the major recommendations of GAC would be a long document and all these were enhanced by the effective personal interaction of GAC with the Commission, especially effective with Robert as chairman.

During this same period Robert served on committees to advise the State Department on international questions involving atomic energy and the Department of Defense regarding areas of interest to the military and especially weapons development. He brought the same knowledge and insight to these committees and inevitably his advice was sought and was respected. It was a new life for him.

In 1947 Oppenheimer, then in residence in Berkeley as professor of theoretical physics, was invited to become the director of the Institute for Advanced Study in Princeton. After many pangs over his separation from California, he accepted. The post offered an opportunity to start a new advanced school of theoretical physics with generous financial support, close ties with subjects of interest to Robert, and a natural place for a person with his broad intellectual scope. In addition, it was close to Washington and meant that he could continue his ties with government much more easily. The Institute had a reputation for very strong work in pure mathematics. Its work in theoretical physics, while excellent under Albert Einstein and John von Neumann, was largely involved in the more mathematical side and there was not much activity in the area of fundamental particles and the origin of nuclear forces. Robert moved quickly to strengthen this area by major staff appointments and made the Institute a world center for young postdoctoral fellows in theoretical physics.

Debris from an atomic bomb had been picked up. It was not a reactor accident. The Soviets had exploded their first atomic bomb.

The Soviet Bomb and the H-Bomb

Early September of 1949 brought the serious news to Robert Oppenheimer and others that some "positive information" had been obtained from the network set up to detect airborne radioactivity. He was asked whether he could become a member of a panel with Vannevar Bush as chairman, to review the findings and assess them. In mid-September the panel met with the specialists in a great vaultlike room, and the results were clear. Debris from an atomic bomb had been picked up. It was not a reactor accident. The Soviets had exploded their first atomic bomb.

Robert Oppenheimer

The question of the H-bomb or Super came before the General Advisory Committee in October 1949. The discussion has been recounted many times and there were many different shades of opinion perhaps not all appreciated fully today.

There was imediate reaction by the public and by the government. The monopoly of the United States was ended. It would, of course, be some time before the Soviet nuclear capability would be significant, but this was a new situation. It called for reexamination of the entire atomic energy program and for reassessment of international relations and objectives. One area in weapon development was singled out for special consideration. This was the thermonuclear weapon based on the nuclear energy released when the heavy isotopes of hydrogen, naturally occurring deuterium and artificially produced tritium, react at very high temperature to produce helium.

The thermonuclear or H-bomb had been worked on almost since the beginning of bomb work. It had been a subject for some of the experimental work done outside the Metallurgical Laboratory in 1942 and it had been a principal subject for the theoretical study conducted under Robert Oppenheimer's guidance in Berkeley in the summer of 1942. During the war a group worked at this project at Los Alamos, difficult as this was under the pressure of the many problems connected with the fission bomb. Work continued on this project after the war but the reduced manpower of the laboratory and later the promising developments of fission weapon development took precedence. One of the principal difficulties was that the early ideas for a "Super" which would couple deuterium into a fission bomb looked less promising as they were examined in greater detail and seemed to require significant quantities of tritium. Tritium had to be produced in nuclear reactors and its production would diminish the production of plutonium.

Robert Oppenheimer

The question of the H-bomb or Super came before the General Advisory Committee in October 1949. The discussion has been recounted many times and there were many different shades of opinion perhaps not all appreciated fully today. Even the question being decided—whether a research program, a crash development program, or any program on the H-bomb—is subject to debate in the public print. However it was, the GAC recommended against a vigorous program to develop the H-bomb. A part of their recommendation was later published, quoted in his hearings by Robert Oppenheimer as follows:

> We all hope that by one means or another, the development of these weapons can be avoided. We are reluctant to see the United States take the initiative in precipitating this development. We are all agreed that it would be wrong at the present moment to commit ourselves to an all out effort towards its development.

To what extent the unpromising state of thermonuclear work at that time contributed is not clear. Also to what extent the imitative nature of the Soviet program up to that time influenced the recommendation is also not clear. Subsequent development made it clear that in this area the Soviets had brilliant men at work.

The recommendation of the GAC, to which there was no dissent, was passed on to the Commission. After long discussion, the Commission reported to President Truman that there was unanimous agreement among the commissioners that this decision, which involved basic national policy on defense posture and

We all hope that by one means or another, the development of these weapons can be avoided. We are reluctant to see the United States take the initiative in precipitating this development. We are all agreed that it would be wrong at the present moment to commit ourselves to an all out effort towards its development.

international relations, must be made by him. There was not an agreed recommendation by the commissioners on what this decision should be.

Their divergent individual views were appended or submitted later. The GAC report was also appended. The commissioners' report was made in early November and the President pondered his decision with further advice from the special committee of the National Security Council set up to consider the production of fissionable material and nuclear weapons. There was vigorous opposition to the GAC recommendation from some scientists, from the military establishment, and from some members of the Joint Congressional Committee on Atomic Energy. In late January, the President instructed the AEC to go ahead with the development of an H-bomb and an announcement was made. The issues became very confused in the public debate in major part because sufficient information for intelligent discussion by ordinary citizens was not available.

top, Edward Teller
bottom, Stan Ulam

There has been a great deal of argument about immediately subsequent events. The records available seem to show that the Commission and the GAC tried to get forward as fast as they could with what appeared to be an unpromising job. There were recriminations from the military and others that the work was not being pushed hard enough.

Robert Oppenheimer

In June of 1951 a meeting was called by Robert Oppenheimer in Princeton to discuss some radical new suggestions which were presented by Edward Teller and for which he and Stanislaus Ulam, with stimulation from von Neumann, were principally responsible. The ideas met with a very favorable reception and it was generally agreed that these were the best ideas yet to be brought into the thermonuclear development. Everyone at this meeting felt that these ideas should be pursued. They were sufficiently different from the original line of the Super that apparently the question was subsequently raised whether following them was really pursuing the President's directive. Nevertheless they were pursued and a large thermonuclear device based on the development of these ideas was exploded in the South Pacific in late 1952.

Robert Oppenheimer's term as a member of the General Advisory Committee expired in 1952 and he had requested that he not be considered for reappointment, believing that some rotation was desirable. It subsequently became known that he had offered to submit his resignation from the GAC earlier following the President's decision. He had, however, been persuaded by Chairman Gordon Dean to stay on at least until the end of his appointment.

From 1951 to 1953 there were several studies sponsored by the Department of Defense and carried out by various universities. These grew out of our participation in the Korean War and concerns

Robert Oppenheimer

expressed over our vulnerability to air attack. Some of these studies considered the possibilities of developing atomic weapons for other than strategic bombing use. The tactical use of nuclear weapons was considered at some length in Project Vista at Caltech. This subject did not find support among those who wished to rely on strategic bombing. The problems of air defense were considered at Project Charles at MIT. Robert Oppenheimer participated in these and other studies as a consultant and as usual with his clarity of mind and background in the subject made major contributions.

In a climate of continued accusations of communists and fellow travelers in government, questions began to be raised in public about Robert Oppenheimer's associations before the war.

Oppenheimer's Security Clearance Questioned

For several years the McCarthy era in Washington had been building up. Several scientists had been called before the House Un-American Activities Committee, among them Edward Condon and Frank Oppenheimer. The climate was quite intolerant of even relatively weak left-wing connections. It was a time of fear for many who had had such connections in the thirties. Both Frank and Robert Oppenheimer were called to testify in 1949 and had been mentioned in other hearings and in various newspaper stories. Robert was asked about people whom he had known and about various incidents that had worried security officers in 1943. Frank was accused of being a member of the Communist party. He first denied this but, testifying under oath before the committee, both he and his wife admitted having been members. This admission made headlines all over the country especially because of Robert's close ties to the government.

In a climate of continued accusations of communists and fellow travelers in government, questions began to be raised in public about Robert Oppenheimer's associations before the war. There were members of the military establishment, both officers and civilians, who put this record together with the recommendations about the H-bomb and the development of tactical nuclear weapons which they found strongly distasteful and came out with strong suspicion of Robert Oppenheimer's motives. Other scientists had been just as much responsible for the recommendations made, but they were not otherwise as vulnerable. In November, 1954, William Borden, a former member of the staff of the Joint Congressional Committee on Atomic Energy addressed a letter to J. Edgar Hoover which contained the following charge and elaborated at length upon it:

> The purpose of this letter is to state my own exhaustively considered opinion based upon years of study of the available classified evidence, that more probably than not J. Robert Oppenheimer is an agent of the Soviet Union.

These charges produced immediate and vigorous action in the government. First there was further FBI investigation and presumably a report. The subject was so inflammatory and the charges so categorical that it soon came to President Eisenhower's urgent attention. Within a month of Borden's letter, the President directed that a "blank wall" be placed between Robert Oppenheimer and any information of a sensitive or classified nature.

The purpose of this letter is to state my own exhaustively considered opinion based upon years of study of the available classified evidence, that more probably than not J. Robert Oppenheimer is an agent of the Soviet Union.

Robert Oppenheimer

When Robert Oppenheimer had retired from the GAC his voluminous and highly classified files in Princeton had been returned to Washington. He still was a consultant to AEC, although not very active and his services had been sought by the Scientific Advisory Committee of the Office of Defense Mobilization. The President's order, of course, stopped these relations, but was in itself an interim measure.

The general manager's letter stated that in view of these charges Robert Oppenheimer's eligibility for access to restricted information was suspended pending final determination.

Further action soon came from AEC in the form of a set of charges in a letter from AEC General Manager Kenneth Nichols. This letter questioned whether Robert Oppenheimer's "...continued employment on Atomic Energy Commission work will endanger the common defense and security and whether such continued employment is clearly consistent with the interest of national security." In brief summary the letter stated that "...these allegations, until disproved, raise questions as to your veracity, conduct and even your loyalty." These charges were deadly serious especially by including Robert's loyalty. To many people they were unbelievable. The specific charges for the most part involved associations with communists or fellow travelers before Los Alamos started. Some of these were people who were subsequently cleared for work on the Manhattan Project. There was the charge that Oppenheimer had contributed to communist-front organizations before the war. There was the charge of negligence in reporting the Haakon Chevalier incident involving an indirect approach to Robert for information regarding the Berkeley project, and of the refusal until ordered to give Chevalier's name, and then not giving the complete story. Chevalier was a Berkeley pre-war friend with left-wing sympathies and the Oppenheimers saw him occasionally after the war. There was also a charge that he had, in the autumn of 1949 and subsequently, strongly opposed the development of the hydrogen bomb. There were numerous other charges but they were all related to these two principal areas. The general manager's letter stated that in view of these charges Robert Oppenheimer's eligibility for access to restricted information was suspended pending final determination. He was offered the opportunity of appearing before an AEC personnel security board if he so stated in writing within thirty days.

Robert Oppenheimer had first been shown a copy of the general manager's letter in draft and told that if he wished to terminate his contract as a consultant to AEC he could do so and "avoid an explicit consideration of the charges." Robert's reply the next day to Chairman Lewis Strauss said in part:

Under the circumstances this would mean that I accept and concur in the view that I am not fit to serve this Government, that I have now served for 12 years. This I cannot do.

> Under the circumstances this would mean that I accept and concur in the view that I am not fit to serve this Government, that I have now served for 12 years. This I cannot do. If I were thus unworthy, I could hardly have served our country as I have tried, or been director of our Institute in Princeton, or have spoken, as on more than one occasion I have found myself speaking, in the name of science and our country.

Robert Oppenheimer

The Security Hearing

Robert Oppenheimer felt that he was forced by the nature of the formal charges to request a hearing. In due course the letter from General Manager Nichols was received. In formal reply Robert sent back a long letter in early March, 1954, which was

> ...in the form of a summary account of relevant aspects of my life in more or less chronological order, in the course of which I shall comment on the specific items in your letter. Through this answer and through the hearings of the personnel security board, which I hereby request, I hope to provide a fair basis upon which the questions posed by your letter may be resolved.

Robert had asked Lloyd Garrison of the New York law firm of Paul, Weiss, Rifkind, Wharton and Garrison to serve as his counsel. Lloyd Garrison had Herbert Marks, former AEC general counsel, as associate. Garrison was assisted by several of his colleagues, especially Samuel Silverman who conducted much of the examination of witnesses. AEC appointed a hearing board consisting of Gordon Gray, president of the University of North Carolina and former Secretary of the Army, as chairman; Ward Evans, professor emeritus of chemistry at Loyola University in Chicago; and Thomas Morgan, chairman of the Board of the Sperry Corporation. The AEC decided to get a lawyer from outside AEC and settled on Roger Robb, an experienced and successful Washington trial lawyer.

The Board convened in early April. 1954, and spent a week reviewing the files and material which had been

What was a serious matter, and what witnesses called to testify in Robert Oppenheimer's behalf were shocked to discover, was the adversary nature of the proceedings.

prepared for it. The hearings actually started on April 12. Lloyd Garrison and his associates had elected not to be cleared for classified information but just prior to the actual hearings had requested clearance in order to be able to be present if classified information should be introduced. This clearance was not obtained before the conclusion of the hearings. According to Lloyd Garrison's comments on the hearings much later, this absence of clearance for restricted data was not really a serious matter.

What was a serious matter, and what witnesses called to testify in Robert Oppenheimer's behalf were shocked to discover, was the adversary nature of the proceedings in contrast to a "hearing." Roger Robb was an experienced trial lawyer and he proceeded in this fashion. Lloyd Garrison and his associates were careful not to discuss the nature of the hearings with new witnesses and a good many of them were surprised to find the extent to which the AEC attorney acted like a prosecutor. Witnesses discovered that information about which they were questioned was often not available to Robert Oppenheimer's counsel or to him. This was not because it involved AEC-restricted data but because allegations reported by the FBI were involved and were therefore not available. Such information would not have been available even if Garrison and his associates had been cleared. They were thus put in the position of having to disprove charges without being able to know and assess the full allegations on which these charges were based. It is often very difficult in a security case to get the full story growing out of some allegation, and indeed this is one of the principal reasons why early security cases for AEC were often sent back more than once to get a more complete investigation.

They were thus put in the position of having to disprove charges without being able to know and assess the full allegations on which these charges were based.

Robert Oppenheimer

Robert Oppenheimer testified at great length and admitted that the story which he had belatedly reported about the Chevalier incident was not true. He acknowledged that his initial account to security officers had been a fabrication and that he had been an "idiot" not to have given a straightforward account promptly.

The hearings were confidential and each witness was cautioned by the Board chairman accordingly. Of the hearings themselves remarkably little was known publicly until they were released by the Commission. This came about because a summary of the hearings had been lost and it was feared that it had fallen into hands that would make it public. Subsequently, it was found, but steps had been started to release the complete transcript (without some passages judged unwise to release because of their relation to classified information) and these steps were not stopped.

The list of witnesses who testified favorably for Robert Oppenheimer included ten members or former members of the GAC, several members of the high command of the Office of Scientific Research and Development, five former AEC commissioners including two former chairmen, three former chairmen of the Research and Development Board of the Department of Defense, General Leslie Groves, John McCloy (Assistant Secretary of War during much of the war), and many colleagues who had worked with Oppenheimer on various studies and committees. There were some, including colleagues who had worked with him in various capacities, who testified unfavorably.

Robert Oppenheimer testified at great length and admitted that the story which he had belatedly reported about the Chevalier incident was not true. He acknowledged that his initial account to security officers had been a fabrication and that he had been an "idiot" not to have given a straightforward account promptly. To Robert's many friends this was a sad incident and not to be excused but it hardly warranted the severe charges made as being generally true. As one witness, Hartley Rowe, said: "I think a man of Dr. Oppenheimer's character is not going to make the same mistake twice. I would say that he was all the more trustworthy for the mistakes he made."

The hearings concluded on May 6, 1954, and toward the end of the month the Board presented its recommendations to the AEC general manager. It was a split vote, with Dr. Ward Evans dissenting, recommending that Robert Oppenheimer's clearance not be reinstated. On the question of loyalty all members concurred that "…he is a loyal citizen." The Board acknowledged the importance of its task noting that "…in a very real sense this case puts the security system of the United States on trial, both as to its procedures and as to substance."

In his minority report, Dr. Evans pointed out that most of the derogatory information which had been presented had been in the hands of the Commission when he had been cleared in 1947. He felt that Oppenheimer was now being investigated again for "practically the same derogatory information." The majority found his conduct in the hydrogen bomb program disturbing. Dr. Evans stated, "He did not hinder the development of the H-bomb and there is absolutely nothing in the testimony to show that he did."

In mid-June AEC General Manager Kenneth Nichols forwarded his recommendations to the Commission, based on the hearings and the conclusions of the Personnel Security Board. He concurred with Gordon Gray and Thomas Morgan that Robert Oppenheimer's clearance should not be

Hartley Rowe said: "I think a man of Dr. Oppenheimer's character is not going to make the same mistake twice. I would say that he was all the more trustworthy for the mistakes he made."

Robert Oppenheimer

Four commissioners, Lewis Strauss, Joseph Campbell, Thomas Murray and Eugene Zuckert, voted to deny clearance for access to restricted data, and Commissioner Henry Smyth voted to reinstate clearance.

reinstated. In so doing he put special emphasis on the Chevalier incident. He also stated that there had been no intention on his part or that of the Board to draw in question any honest opinion expressed by Oppenheimer on the H-bomb. It is not easy to square this view with the statement of the original charges or the positions of several witnesses who testified adversely on Oppenheimer's views. Finally, the general manager stated that Oppenheimer's services had been utilized on only three occasions since he left the GAC and that it was unlikely that "...the AEC, even if the question of his security clearance had not arisen, would have utilized his services to a markedly greater extent in the next few years." No mention was made of the Board's finding with which all members agreed, that Robert Oppenheimer was a loyal citizen.

The case next came before the Atomic Energy Commission. The commissioners had before them all of the material already considered including the transcript of the hearings, the findings and recommendations of the Personnel Security Board, the briefs of Oppenheimer's counsel and the recommendation of the general manager as well as the FBI files. The commissioners gave a decision on June 29, 1954, one day before Robert Oppenheimer's consultant contract with AEC expired. Four commissioners, Lewis Strauss, Joseph Campbell, Thomas Murray and Eugene Zuckert, voted to deny clearance for access to restricted data, and Commissioner Henry Smyth voted to reinstate clearance.

Commissioners Strauss, Zuckert, and Campbell prepared a majority statement which emphasized the Chevalier incident and Oppenheimer's associates dating back to before the war. Comments on the charge about his opinions on the H-bomb were not included except for an incident involving a missing letter from Glenn Seaborg. No statement was made about his loyalty or the conclusions of the Gray Board that he was a loyal citizen. It was noted at the start, however, that "The Atomic Energy Act of 1946 lays upon the Commissioners the duty to reach a determination as to 'character, associations and loyalty' of the individuals engaged in the work of the Commission." Commissioner Zuckert submitted an additional concurring opinion and Commissioner Murray submitted a separate opinion stating his reasons for voting that clearance should be denied.

No statement was made about his loyalty or the conclusions of the Gray Board that he was a loyal citizen.

Commissioner Smyth submitted a dissenting opinion, reviewing the principal incidents and points that had been raised in the majority opinion. His conclusions were quite opposite. He wrote:

> Character and associations are important only insofar as they bear on the possibility that secret information will be improperly revealed. In my opinion the most important evidence in this regard is the fact that there is no indication in the entire record that Dr. Oppenheimer has ever divulged any secret information. The past 15 years of his life have been investigated and reinvestigated. For much of the last 11 years he has been under actual surveillance, his movements watched, his conversations noted, his mail and telephone calls checked. This professional review of his actions has been supplemented by enthusiastic amateur help from powerful personal enemies.

Robert Oppenheimer

On the H-bomb which he considered to be the subject of the most important allegations of the general manager's letter, Commissioner Smyth said that he was "...not surprised to find that the evidence does not support these allegations in any way." He concludes that "Dr. Oppenheimer's employment will not endanger the common defense and security and will be clearly consistent with the interests of national security. I prefer the positive statement that Dr. Oppenheimer's further employment will continue to strengthen the United States."

This decision marked the end of Robert Oppenheimer's work as an adviser to the government and any participation in or access to classified work.

This decision marked the end of Robert Oppenheimer's work as an adviser to the government and any participation in or access to classified work. After having contributed so much during the war as director of Los Alamos and so much after the war in many different capacities, his contribution was now completely ended. Robert was deeply wounded and hurt but much less bitter than almost anyone else would have been. Scientists in all the western world rallied to his support and continued to support him for the remainder of his life.

Everywhere people inquired, "How could this happen in the United States?" Some were inclined to blame those who opposed his views about the H-bomb, but in fact these charges had been excluded both by the Board and by the Commission. Others were inclined to blame those who had become Robert's enemies for one reason or another, often because his lucid mind sometimes gave expression in a very sharp tongue. Still others blamed the whole climate of the McCarthy era which unfortunately was just at its peak in the spring of 1954. No one of these can be singled out as a principal reason for what happened but it is probably fair to say that, if the country had not been paralyzed by the witch hunts and the fear of communists, none of the other factors would have been sufficient to make things come out the way they did. In a sense Robert Oppenheimer was an unfortunate victim of the national paroxysm of this witch hunt.

The Gray Board had remarked when it started its hearings that Robert Oppenheimer's case put the security system on trial. One can only conclude that the security system did not stand the test. The result was a gross miscarriage of justice for a man who had made some of the greatest contributions to our country and who was one of the world's intellectual leaders. It would be hard to maintain that the case was conducted as stated by AEC procedures:

The result was a gross miscarriage of justice for a man who had made some of the greatest contributions to our country and who was one of the world's intellectual leaders.

> The acts of each case must be carefully weighed and determination made in the light of all the information presented, whether favorable or unfavorable. The judgment of responsible persons as to the integrity of the individuals should be considered. The decision as to security clearance is an overall, common sense judgment, made after consideration of all the relevant information as to whether or not there is risk that the granting of security clearance would endanger the common defense or security.

The security system of AEC was not set up for the prosecutor-type tactics that were used in the hearings. Probably the only place for such tactics is in an open

Robert Oppenheimer

Perhaps nothing could have been done by Oppenheimer's counsel to avoid entrapment of Oppenheimer and other witnesses whose memories of details of events twelve years or more past were not as reliable as written records or transcriptions.

court of law. Perhaps nothing could have been done by Oppenheimer's counsel to avoid entrapment of Oppenheimer and other witnesses whose memories of details of events twelve years or more past were not as reliable as written records or transcriptions. Perhaps, as Joseph Volpe had recommended, a tough criminal lawyer was needed by Robert's counsel to counter such tactics.

To conduct such hearings in private and to have the information available to the Board not more fully available to counsel for the defendant made it almost impossible to achieve a fair conclusion at the height of a period of national apathy and a period of fear of the use of innuendo and smear by parts of our government. The nature of security for classified information makes it difficult to conduct hearings openly. While no information can be kept secret indefinitely and while much is classified that need not be, still there is and there will in the future be need for closely guarded national secrets. It is very doubtful that we have a security system that can provide fair hearings and decisions for an individual who is brought up at a time such as the spring of 1954. It is not clear whether at that time Robert Oppenheimer might not have been better off before the McCarthy committee or the Jenner committee. At least what came out would been currently subjected to public scrutiny and might have helped to bring our nation to its senses somewhat sooner.

Continuing at Princeton

Robert Oppenheimer returned to his work as director of the Institute for Advanced Study in Princeton. The liveliness and intensity which had characterized his activities before were gone. He was greatly changed. In recent years so much of his effort had been devoted to his advisory activities and his interests in international cooperation that he had not personally been really active in particle-physics research. Now he lacked the strength and perhaps the interest to throw himself completely into this work. He felt, probably rightly, that intense participation was for younger men. The Institute under his directorship had become the leading center for theoretical physics. He had a distinguished senior staff with Freeman Dyson, Abraham Pais, George Placzek, Tsung-Dao Lee, and Cheng Ning Yang, in addition to Einstein and von Neumann, who had been there for many years. The large school of postdoctoral fellows which he had developed was in full bloom and not only did he continue to encourage them but his remarkable ability to stimulate young physicists was an important part of its success. Princeton was a center of intense activity and much of it was due to Robert's stimulating leadership of discussions and seminars. His clarity, insight, and

Robert Oppenheimer

capability for summation of the most complicated and difficult situations always played an important role whenever he was present. He was always in demand as a discussion leader or summary speaker for the important international meetings which had really grown up from small conferences that he had started after the war.

For many years Robert Oppenheimer had been in great demand as a speaker. He had talked to widely different audiences on subjects which included "The Scientist in Society," "The Encouragement of Science," "Physics in a Contemporary World," "Atomic Weapons and American Policy," and "Atomic Energy as a Contemporary Problem." In 1955 he collected these and published them under the title of another of the talks, "The Open Mind," in which he pointed out the need in a democracy for information if the citizens are to arrive at sensible conclusions. These talks were all cogent and beautifully presented. After 1954 his interests turned more toward the relationship of science to other subjects including the arts, and its development and impact on our society. In late 1953 he had delivered the Reith Lectures over the home service of the British Broadcasting Corporation and these were published in 1954 with some added notes and appendices. These six lectures covered parts of science from Newton to the present, the relationship of the sciences and a concluding talk on "Science and Man's Community." They carried the appropriate title "Science and the Common Understanding." These lectures were typically Robert Oppenheimer in their breadth of vision, depth of understanding, and beauty of expression.

After 1954 his interests turned more toward the relationship of science to other subjects including the arts, and its development and impact on our society.

In succeeding years Robert gave many talks principally on subjects covered in his Reith Lectures and especially on some of the fundamental dilemmas of physics but including many other topics as well. Three of these given at McMaster University in 1962 were published under the title "The Flying Trapeze: Three Crises for Physicists." There were a great many lectures given in the late fifties and early sixties which were not published. Many of these were given at universities where students, faculty, and others gave him standing ovations. In addition, he appeared in a long television interview with Edward R. Murrow which attracted wide attention and showed clearly his reflective mood in these years. Wherever he went he was recognized and it was impossible for him to travel in this country or in Europe without strangers coming up to greet him and wish him well.

In 1960 the International Atomic Energy Agency of which Sterling Cole, formerly a member of the Joint Congressional Committee on Atomic Energy, was director general, appointed Robert Oppenheimer representative to an international conference. In 1961, after Kennedy became President, he began to be accepted a little by Washington. There was greater sympathy and appreciation from some of the President's close advisers. He visited Latin America to lecture under the sponsorship of the Organization of American States. His visit and his lectures attracted great attention and enthusiastic comment. He was invited to attend a dinner at the White House for Nobel Laureates as a special guest. In the spring of 1963, Chairman Glenn Seaborg told him that the AEC was awarding the Fermi Prize to him. Although announced earlier the formal award by the President

Wherever he went he was recognized and it was impossible for him to travel this country or in Europe without strangers coming up to greet him and wish him well.

Robert Oppenheimer

was scheduled for December 2, the anniversary of the first self-sustaining chain reaction. The President's assassination in Dallas threw all plans into doubt and confusion, including these. But President Johnson decided that the award ceremony would go ahead at the White House as planned. Robert was deeply moved. It was a recognition long deserved but to which there was still strong opposition. In his reply, Robert said, "I think it is just possible, Mr. President, that it has taken some charity and some courage for you to make this award today."

The late fifties and early sixties were difficult ones too for his wife and children. The hearings had been an ordeal for them, especially for Kitty, who was present with him most of the time. It was hard for the children who could not understand what it was all about except that everything seemed unfair. The hearings meant that they were separated from their parents for much of the spring. Later Kitty was plagued by recurrent illness which bothered her for many years. Robert acquired

Oppenheimer receiving the Fermi Award from President Johnson, Dec., 1963

48

a place on the ocean in the Virgin Islands and the whole family spent much of the early summer there as well as shorter periods during the year. It was a welcome respite from a busy life and so much publicity, and it gave an opportunity for the family to be close together again.

Oppenheimer's Achievements

Robert's health had never been really good and for many years he seemed to live on nervous energy. This now deserted him and he became increasingly frail. He had for many years been subject to a severe rasping cough. In early 1966 it was discovered that he had throat cancer. There was an operation and extended radiation treatments. For a time, Robert could still travel around but he resigned as director and became senior professor at the Institute. Before long there was recurrence of his disease and it became clear that the end was not far off. Though weak, he kept his clarity of mind and, as much as his strength would bear, he enjoyed seeing friends and remembering earlier and more pleasant times. The end came on Saturday, February 18, 1967.

Oppenheimers on a visit to Japan in 1960

Robert Oppenheimer

All spoke of the feeling which they all shared of how exciting it had been to work with him.

A memorial service was held in Princeton on February 25. Hans Bethe, Henry Smyth and George Kennan gave moving summaries of Robert Oppenheimer's career as they knew him and his many accomplishments. A memorial session of the American Physical Society was held at the spring meeting in Washington at which Serber, Weisskopf, Pais, and Seaborg spoke of the various phases of Robert Oppenheimer's very productive career. All spoke of the feeling which they all shared of how exciting it had been to work with him. Rabi, who was unable to be present and who had known him since the early days in Germany, wrote a penetrating and glowing introduction to the published accounts.

Abraham Pais, his close colleague at the Institute in Princeton said:

Any single one of the following contributions would have marked Oppenheimer out as a pre-eminent scientist: his own research work in physics; his influence as a teacher; his leadership at Los Alamos; the growth of the Institute for Advanced Study as a leading center of theoretical physics under his directorship; and his efforts to promote a more common understanding of science. When all is combined we honor Oppenheimer as a great leader of science. When all is interwoven with the dramatic events that centered around him we remember Oppenheimer as one of the most remarkable personalities of this century.

Robert Oppenheimer

Robert Oppenheimer's thoughts on science and its relation to man and society are shown in the concluding remarks of his Reith Lectures:

We know that our work is rightly both an instrument and an end. A great discovery is a thing of beauty; and our faith—our binding, quiet faith—is that knowledge is good and good in itself. It is also an instrument; it is an instrument for our successors, who will use it to probe elsewhere and more deeply; it is an instrument for technology, for the practical arts, and for man's affairs. So it is with us as scientists; so it is with us as men. We are at once instrument and end, discoverers and teachers, actors and observers. We understand, as we hope others understand, that in this there is a harmony between knowledge in the sense of science, that specialized and general knowledge, which it is our purpose to uncover, and the community of man. We, like all men, are among those who bring a little light to the vast unending darkness of man's life and world. For us as for all men, change and eternity, specialization and unity, instrument and final purpose, community and individual man alone, complementary each to the other, both require and define our bonds and our freedom.

We understand, as we hope others understand, that in this there is a harmony between knowledge in the sense of science, that specialized and general knowledge, which it is our purpose to uncover, and the community of man.

About the Author

Robert F. Bacher was born in 1905. He earned a B.S. and Ph. D. in physics from the University of Michigan. He pursued teaching and research at various universities, including Michigan, California Institute of Technology, Massachusetts Institute of Technology, Columbia and Cornell. After working at the Radiation Laboratory at M.I.T., he joined the Los Alamos Laboratory. After the war he returned to Caltech, where he was professor of physics and head of the division of physics, mathematics and astronomy 1949-1962 and Provost 1962-1970. He was a member of the Atomic Energy Commission from 1946 to 1949 and of the President's Scientific Advisory Committee from 1953 to 1955 and 1957 to 1960. He is Professor Emeritus at Caltech.

Acknowledgements

Special thanks go to Gloria Sharp for design of this monograph and of the series, *The Los Alamos Story*, and for her invaluable technical support. Thanks also to the J. Robert Oppenheimer Memorial Committee of Los Alamos for reprint rights of this article which appeared in 1974. The photographs are from the archives of the Los Alamos National Laboratory, of the Los Alamos Historical Society, or both.

Robert Oppenheimer

Other Los Alamos Historical Society books
about the Manhattan Project

A Guide to the Nuclear Arms Control Treaties
by David B. Thomson

Gatekeeper to Los Alamos
by Nancy Cook Steeper

In August 1945
by Paul Numerof

Inside Box 1663
by Eleanor Jette

Life Within Limits
by Eleanor Stone Roensch

Los Alamos: Beginning of an Era 1943-1945
LASL Publication Reprint

Manhattan District History
Edith C. Truslow, editor

Norris Bradbury
Virginia Ebinger, editor

Plutonium Metallurgy at Los Alamos, 1943-1945
by Edward F. Hammel

Remembering Los Alamos: World War II
(Video or DVD)

Secrets! of a Los Alamos Kid, 1946–1953
by Kristin Embry Litchman

Standing By and Making Do: Women of Wartime Los Alamos
Jane S. Wilson and Charlotte Serber, editors

Tales of Los Alamos
by Bernice Brode

The Secret Project Notebook
by Carolyn Reeder, 2005
(for young readers)

*Twilight Time:
A Soldier's Role in the Manhattan Project at Los Alamos*
by Ralph C. Sparks

Robert Oppenheimer

Robert Oppenheimer